ISSUES IN OUR WORLD

IMMIGRATION

Ruth Wilson

Aladdin / Watts
London • Sydney

ABOUT THIS BOOK

IMMIGRATION is the process of people moving to live in a new country. Why do they move? What happens when they do? This book looks at the history of immigration and the laws behind it. It also examines how immigration affects us all.

© Aladdin Books Ltd 2007
Produced by Aladdin Books Ltd
2/3 Fitzroy Mews, London W1T 6DF

ISBN 978–07496–7485–4

First published in 2007 by

Franklin Watts	Franklin Watts Australia
338 Euston Road	Level 17/207 Kent Street
London NW1 3BH	Sydney NSW 2000

Franklin Watts is a division of Hachette Children's Books.

Designers: Flick, Book Design and Graphics
Pete Bennett – PBD
Editors: Harriet Brown / Katie Dicker
Picture research: Brian Hunter Smart

The author, Ruth Wilson, is a researcher and writer on refugees and other issues. She has worked with the Refugee Council, the Refugee Arrivals Project and other refugee agencies.

Printed in Malaysia
All rights reserved

A CIP catalogue record for this book is available from the British Library.

Dewey Classification: 304.8'2

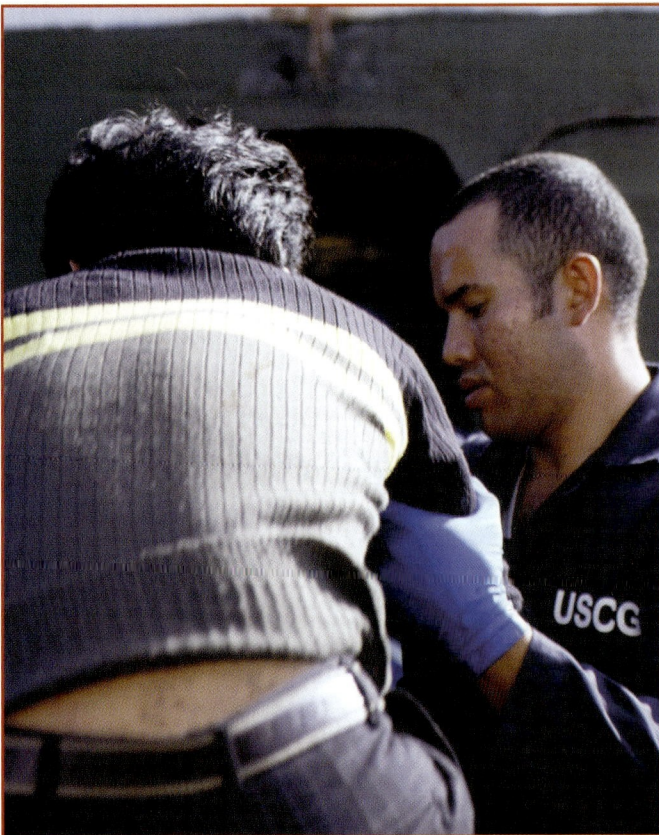

CONTENTS

3

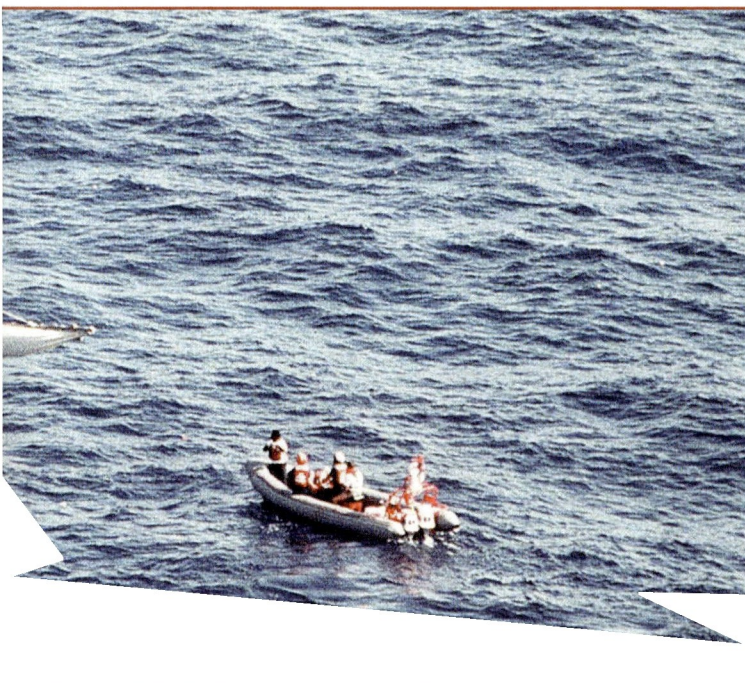

INTRODUCTION

The words 'immigration' and 'asylum' are often in the news. Wars and disasters force people to move away. Sometimes, companies employ immigrants who work for very little money.

Our world is constantly changing as people move from place to place. This book takes a look at what is going on behind the headlines. Why do people move? Where do they come from? How do they decide which country to go to?

Many people leave their country to begin a new life somewhere else.

There are probably many immigrants living and working in your area.

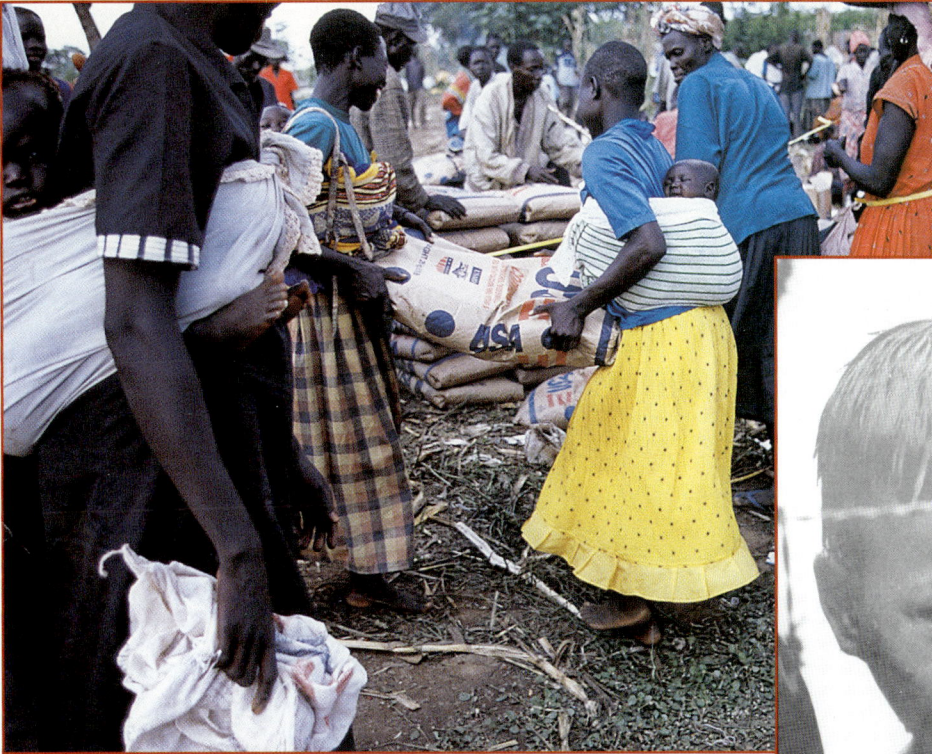

Up to ten million people move each year in search of a better life.

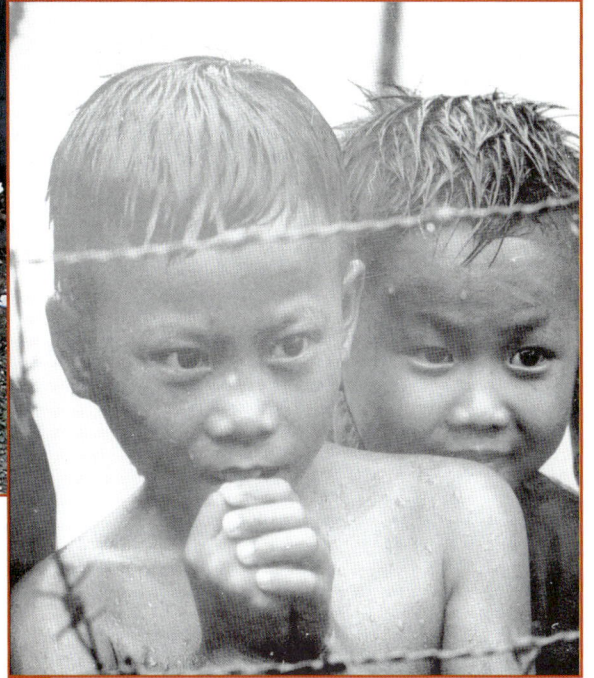

Many immigrants are children.

IMMIGRATION

The word 'immigration' is used to describe the arrival of people who come to live or work in a new country. Some people go abroad to work for a few months each year. Other people travel to a different country each day, to go to work. Immigration can also be caused by wars or disasters.

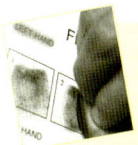

A history of travelling

People have always looked for a better life in other countries. Over the years, traders, explorers and invaders have all travelled around the world.

Many women and children are now moving, too. In this book we explain why this can be dangerous (see pages 30-33). Sometimes, governments try to stop people from entering their country. We take a look at what countries do to stop migration (see pages 36-38). We also look at what people do when they arrive in a new country – and why it is sometimes difficult to return home again.

5

WHAT IS IMMIGRATION?

Immigration means entering a new country to live. Immigrants often come to find work or a better way of life. Many different words are used to describe people who move to a different country.

Words used to describe immigrants

Asylum seekers – people who ask for protection in another country.

Contract/seasonal workers – workers who stay in a country to do a particular piece of work.

Economic migrants – anyone who travels legally to work.

Illegal immigrants – people who do not have the official papers needed to stay and work in a country.

Professionals – people such as nurses, doctors, teachers and scientists. Some go to work for large organisations who employ people in many countries.

Refugees – people who move away in search of refuge (safety).

Settlers – people who live permanently in a new place.

Many illegal immigrants take great risks to reach a new country.

A GROWING PROBLEM

The number of immigrants has more than doubled in the past 35 years. However, the world's population has also increased a lot during this time. But in the next 20-30 years, this growth in world population is likely to slow down. This means that the number of immigrants will probably stay below 3% (see graph, right).

It is estimated that up to ten million people move between countries across the world each year. However, most of these people are on short-term trips. They are not thought to be 'immigrants'.

World population
(in millions)

■ Non-migrants
■ Migrants

	1965	2000	2050
Non-migrants	3,258	5,882	8,770
Migrants	75 (2.3%)	175 (2.9%)	230 (2.6%)

These people are moving from Haiti to find a better life in the USA.

MOVING AROUND

All countries of the world are affected by immigration. In some countries, people leave (or emigrate). In immigration countries, people arrive to live and work. Some countries experience both of these things.

In Argentina, for example, immigrants arrive looking for work. However, because the country is poor, many people are trying to leave. Sometimes, people travel through a country on their way to somewhere else. We call this a 'transit' country.

7

FROM PLACE TO PLACE

Every year, over two million people move from developing parts of the world (such as Africa and Asia) to developed areas (such as Europe and the USA). Even more people just move from one developing country to another. A lot of these people move within the same continent.

Top five immigration nations

USA	38.4 million
Russian Federation	12.1 million
Germany	10.1 million
Ukraine	6.8 million
France	6.5 million

The most common migrants are Chinese (35 million) Indian (20 million) or Filipino (7 million). There are around 23.7 million displaced people worldwide.

Figures for 2005

Map of some of the main migration movements.

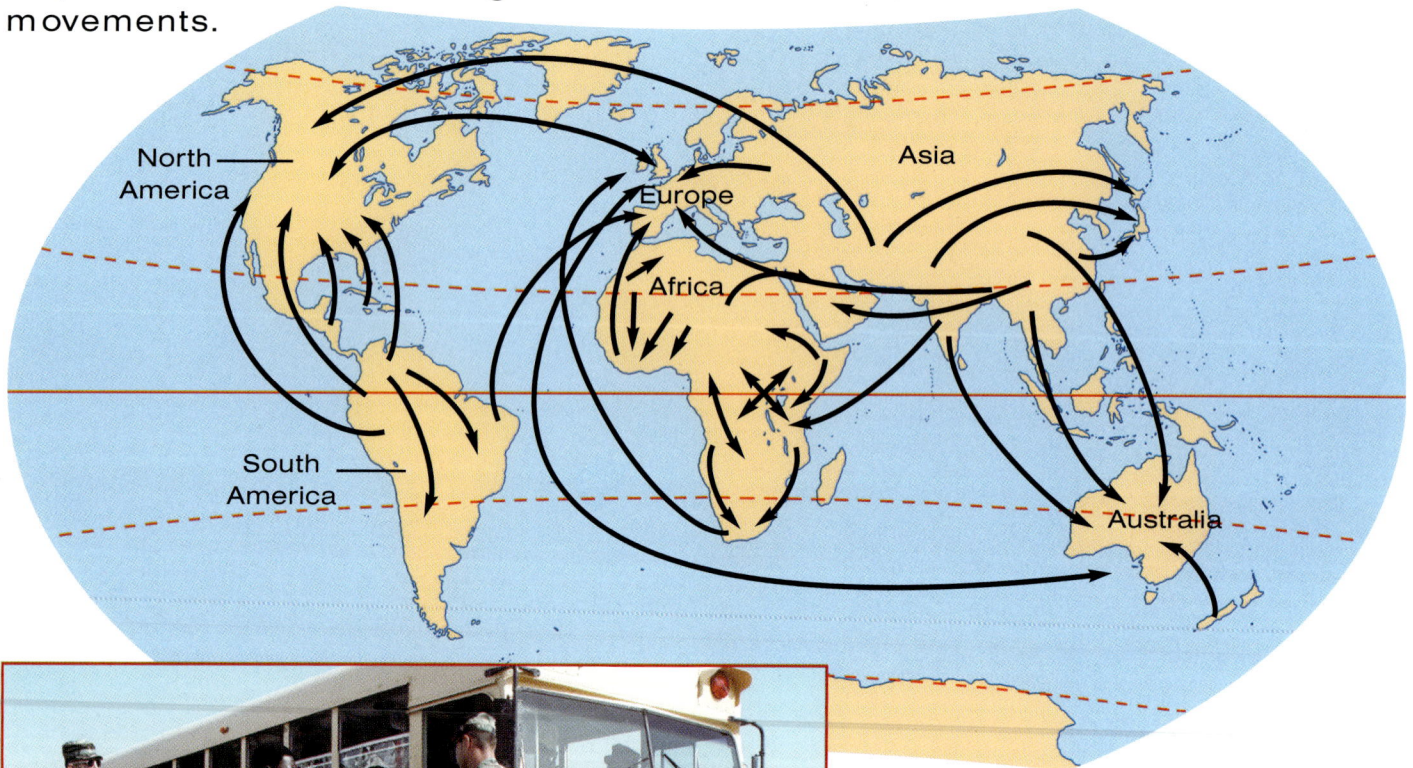

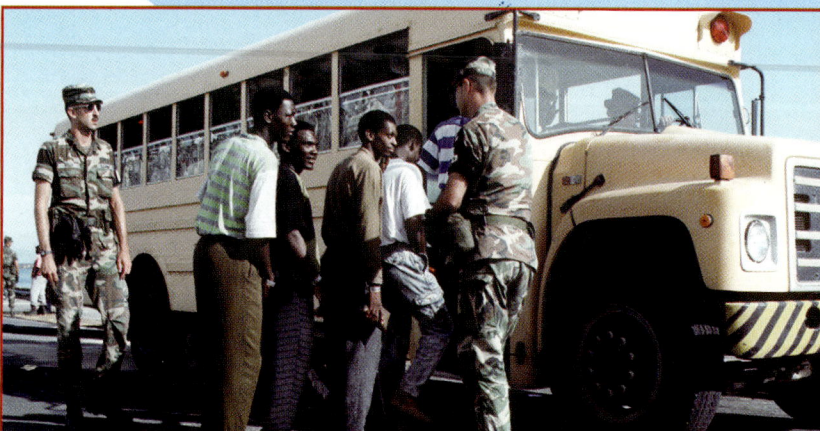

People are always moving in different directions around the world.

8

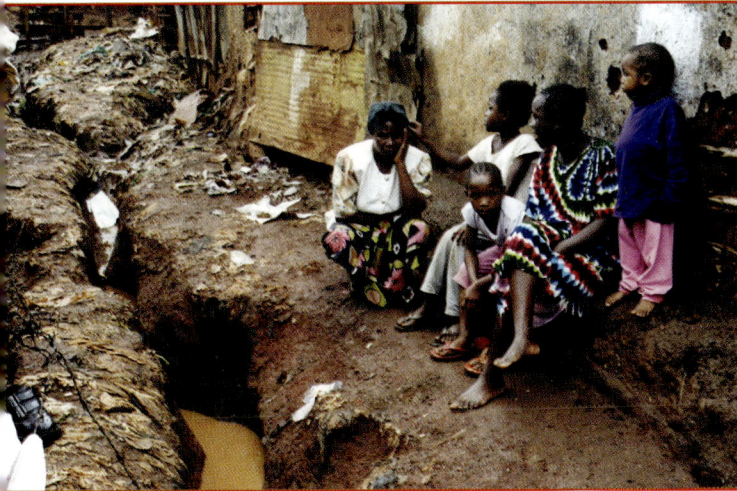

Some people migrate
to escape poverty.

REASONS TO MOVE

Choosing to leave your home and your country is a big decision. You need to have good reasons to leave your friends and family to start a new life somewhere else.

Because countries can be rich or poor, many people move to improve their way of life. Others want to escape from war, bad government, or environmental problems such as drought.

THE POVERTY TRAP

In some developing countries there is not enough work to go round. However, often the poorest people don't have the knowledge or the money they need to move away.

THE GLOBAL ECONOMY

In today's world, countries buy and sell goods from each other. Companies also look for people who work for very little money.

In the 1970s, there was a lot of work in countries that produced oil (such as Saudi Arabia and Iran). Then in the 1980s, more jobs became available in Taiwan, Singapore, South Korea and Hong Kong. When the Soviet empire broke up in the 1990s, even more countries were created. China is now an important country in world trade, too.

9

A short history

Before the 19th century, most people stayed in the place where they were born. In the 19th century, however, new industries and cities developed in Europe. People found they could no longer live off the land so they moved to the cities. But there was not enough work to go round. Many people left Europe to live in North America. Since then migration has steadily increased.

? Advantages and disadvantages of immigration

Disadvantages

There is not enough work, so immigrants are often unemployed.

Immigrants take the jobs of local people.

Because immigrants work for low pay, other wages become lower.

Immigrants try not to pay taxes that raise money for a country.

Immigrants use services that cost the government a lot of money.

There isn't room for more people.

Immigration can lead to racism and violence. Some immigrants commit crimes.

Immigrants are often needed in their own country.

Advantages

Immigrants often do unpopular jobs. They can also be useful if they are skilled workers.

Immigrants create work. They use public transport and go shopping. Many have their own businesses.

Immigrants work for little money. This keeps the cost of living down. They also help local people to get better jobs. Immigrant nannies, for example, help mothers to work.

Immigrants help to raise money for their new country over time. Most immigrants are employed.

Developed countries often have lots of old people and very few young. They need people to work and make money for the country.

Immigrants bring new customs and traditions to a country, making it a more interesting place to live.

Many immigrants send money home. This is a great help to the country they were born in.

CHOOSING TO MOVE

Most immigrants choose to move away. However, others run away from their country because of war, famine or other difficulties. This is called forced migration.

A drought can cause people to move away.

CHOICES TO MAKE

Immigrants need to prepare for their new life. They need to find out where they will be able to work. Doctors, nurses and teachers are needed in many parts of the world. However, some countries do not allow you to work if you have taken different professional exams. Immigrants may find they have to change their job.

Sometimes, skilled workers have to take a low-paid job. Immigrants also need to find out how much they will earn and what their new life will cost. Some jobs may be well paid, but the new country might be expensive to live in.

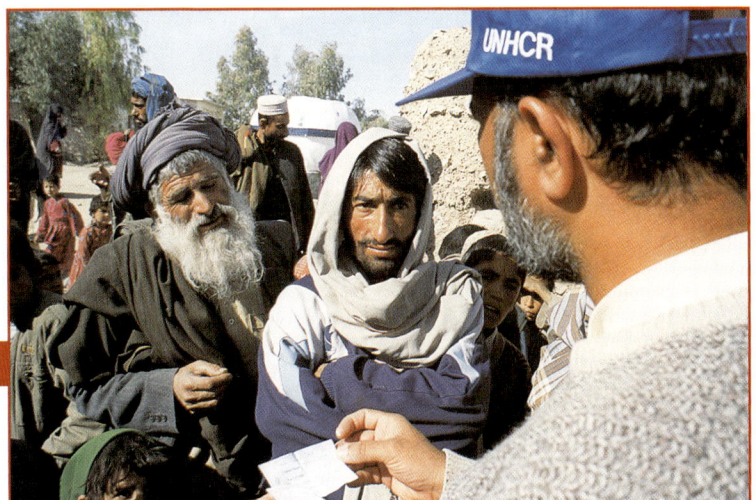

These refugees are trying to move to a new country.

Immigrants also have to think about how they are going to travel.

Paperwork is also needed.

Language barrier

People often go to a country where they speak the same language. Some languages are easier than others. English is spoken by many people.

Sometimes, it can be difficult to get official documents. Many people travel with false papers, or go to another country secretly, with no papers at all.

The costs

Immigrants need to pay for the journey and they need enough money when they arrive. Some people have their ticket paid by their employer. Others save up for years. Some people pay smugglers to get them into a country. This can put them in debt. Many people end up working for gangs and earn very little money, or none at all.

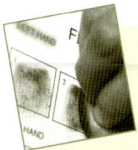

A migrant's story

Artan is 23 years old, and from Albania. When he left school there was little work so he decided to migrate, and crossed illegally into Macedonia. He couldn't find any work there, however, and found he'd spent all his money. Artan decided to go to Greece, where the pay was better. He ended up working on a farm for a few months and saved some money. But then the police found he had no documents and he was sent back to Albania.

Local contacts

Many people travel to a country where a friend or a relative is living. These people may be able to help them to get a job. There may also be immigrants living nearby who speak the same language and can give advice. Sometimes, people travel short distances to work in another country and come home each night or at the weekends.

An immigrant invented 'hotmail' – an email service on the internet.

Many big cities have a Chinatown that is home to lots of Chinese immigrants.

MAKING A BIG SUCCESS

Some immigrants are very successful. Sabeer Bhatia grew up in Bangalore, India. After studying in the USA, he worked for a computer firm. Sabeer invented hotmail. This is a simple and free way to email using the internet. He sold the idea to Microsoft for a reported US$400 million.

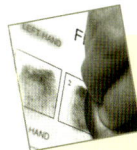

A family of migrants

Winston left Barbados when he was 14. He went to the UK to join his mother who had moved there ten years earlier. Winston was educated in the UK, before he moved to Guyana to teach. He married a Guyanese woman, Andrea. They returned to the UK, but may move back to Barbados.

13

FORCED TO MIGRATE

When refugees move from their country, they cannot return because they are in danger. This may be because they are treated badly because of their race, religion, nationality or political views.

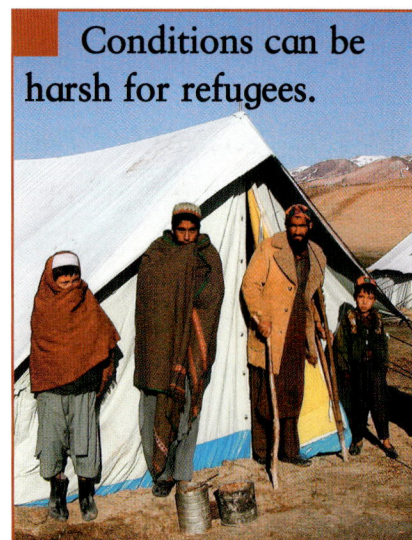

Conditions can be harsh for refugees.

In the past 50 years, millions of people have been given asylum (protection) in another country.

Refugee rights

In 1948, the United Nations (UN) agreed the Universal Declaration of Human Rights. This law says that people who are treated badly must be able to leave their country and seek safety elsewhere.

In 1951, the Office of the UN High Commissioner for Refugees (UNHCR) was created to help refugees. In the same year, the UN made an agreement that outlined the rights of refugees. This is often called the Geneva Convention.

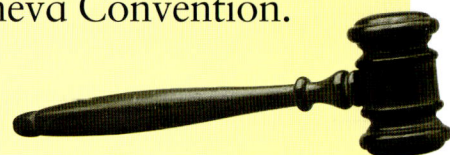

Governments and international organisations talk about immigration issues in Geneva, Switzerland.

FORCED TO MOVE

Refugees come from all over the world. Many refugees are from countries where there are wars or bad governments. Lots of people may try to move away in a short period of time. However, not everyone is able to escape. Some governments imprison or even kill people who are against them.

Israel and Afghanistan

When the country Israel was created in 1948, 80% of Palestinians had to leave. There are now over four million Palestinian refugees. More than four million refugees have also fled from Afghanistan. This is because of a war that lasted over 20 years.

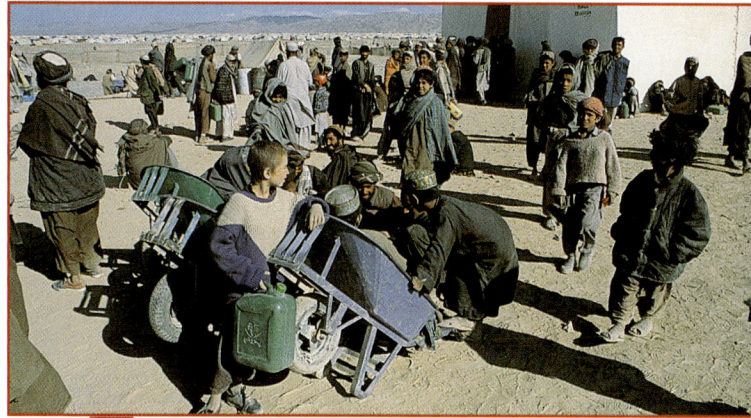

Many Afghan refugees have gone to Pakistan.

Other countries

Since 1997, war has badly affected the Democratic Republic of the Congo. Thousands of people have been killed or injured and many have moved away.

More than 100,000 Liberians have also moved from their country. Between 1997 and 2003, the president imprisoned anyone who criticised his government. The president has now been forced to live in Nigeria, but the situation in Liberia is still difficult.

Many refugees also come from Iraq. At least 400,000 Iraqis now live in 90 countries. They moved to escape war and their former leader Saddam Hussein.

15

Where refugees live

Iran	1.3 million
Pakistan	1.2 million
Germany	980,000
Tanzania	690,000
USA	485,000
Serbia and Montenegro	350,000
	(Figures from 2002)

DEVELOPED COUNTRIES

In 2002, the five developed countries with the highest number of asylum seekers were the UK (110,700), USA (81,100), Germany (71,000), France (50,800) and Canada (33,400). If we compare the number of asylum seekers with a country's population, however, Austria has the most. In 2002, Austria had 4.6 applicants for every 1,000 people.

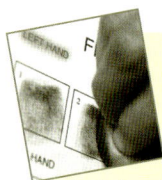

Developed nations are popular with asylum seekers.

Refugee stories

Tiawan Gongloe is a leading Liberian human rights lawyer. He was arrested for talking about violence in his country. He was beaten very badly. Luckily a human rights group helped Tiawan and his family to leave Liberia. He is now a refugee in the USA.

Golnaz left Iran when she was 20. Her father was in prison for his political views and a number of her friends had been shot for challenging the government. Golnaz had money and a passport. She decided to go to Sweden, to seek asylum.

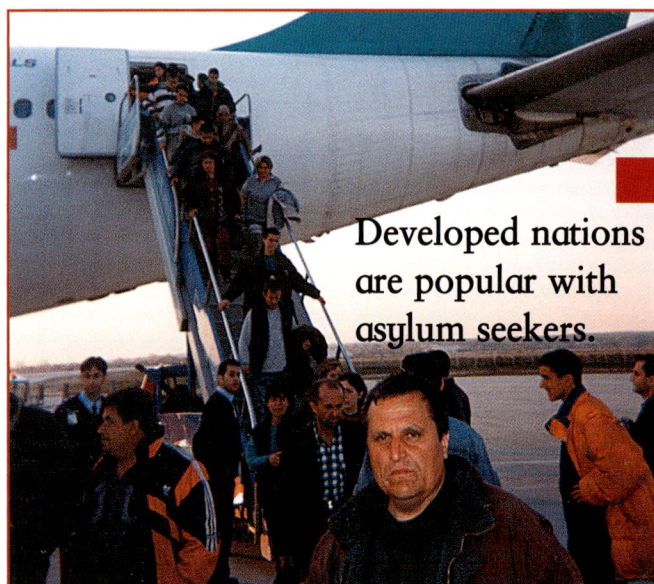

GOVERNMENT VIEWS

Some countries choose to take many refugees. Others don't have any choice. If their country shares a border with a war zone, it is hard to stop people coming in.

In recent years, however, many countries have closed their doors to asylum seekers. They see refugees as a threat or a burden. A number of countries have laws limiting the rights of asylum seekers. Some people think these laws are unfair.

Sometimes, refugees abuse the system. They ask for asylum as a way to find a job, even if they are not trying to escape from their country. This makes it harder for other refugees to find safety.

FAMOUS REFUGEES

There are many famous refugees. The physicist Albert Einstein (left), the philosopher Hannah Arendt, and the filmstar Andy Garcia were all refugees.

Miriam Makeba

In the 1950s, the South African singer Miriam Makeba appeared in a TV documentary. She criticised the way the government of South Africa was treating black people. Afterwards, the South African government said she could not live in the country any more. However, Makeba was able to return to South Africa in the 1990s because the government had changed.

The Dalai Lama

The Dalai Lama is the head of state and spiritual leader of the Tibetan people. When the Chinese invaded Tibet, the Dalai Lama escaped to India in 1959. Many refugees followed him there.

Edward Said

When Israel was created in 1948, Edward Said and his family were forced to move to Egypt. Said later moved to the USA, where he became a professor at a university.

For many years Said argued about the situation of Palestinians. He also helped to set up an orchestra which brought Palestinian and Israeli musicians together. Said's books have been translated into 26 languages. However, his views brought him many enemies. Said died in 2003.

In 1989, the Dalai Lama was given the Nobel Peace Prize for his work on human rights.

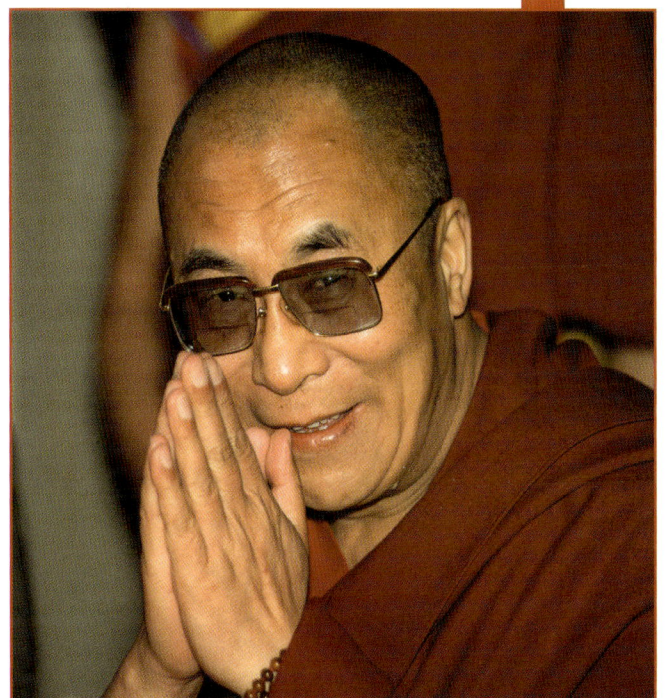

17

MAKING THE JOURNEY

Aeroplanes have made it easier for legal immigrants to travel. However, some asylum seekers have much more difficult journeys. Migration has become big business. Some people offer to help immigrants to travel and to find a job. This may be legal, but sometimes it is not. Travelling with illegal smugglers can be very dangerous.

The journey to a new country can be long and difficult.

Aeroplanes are a useful form of transport for some immigrants.

SMUGGLING

Smugglers make money by getting people into countries. Some give people false papers or transport them hidden in lorries. Others pay officials to help them. In Russia, around 450,000 illegal migrants are trying to travel westward. Chinese gangs also smuggle people. This can be dangerous.

In 2000, 58 Chinese migrants were discovered dead in a lorry at Dover, UK. They had suffocated because they were trapped in the lorry. Other gangs arrange boats from North Africa to Spain. Around 200 people drown each year swimming the last part of this route.

TRAFFICKING

Between one and two million people are illegally trafficked each year. Traffickers threaten people or trick them into travelling. Most of these immigrants are women and children. They end up working in the sex industry, or as slaves for other people.

Thousands of people are smuggled across borders each year. The conditions can be very dangerous.

MEXICO TO THE USA

The border between the USA and Mexico is one of world's most popular crossings. Between 1998 and 2001, more than 1,500 people died trying to cross to the USA. Most of them died from heatstroke and dehydration as they crossed the desert and the Rio Grande river.

There are a lot of police on the US side of the border. High fences and helicopter patrols are also used. However, the border is very long and it is impossible to control all of it. Since the US terrorist attacks of 2001, however, there are new, tougher penalties for anyone caught entering illegally.

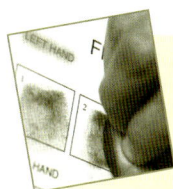

Smuggled to safety

Mohammed fled Afghanistan when his brother was forced to fight for the Taliban. Mohammed drove to the border, walked for three days towards Turkey and then into Bulgaria. He hid on a train to Greece and then paid smugglers for the final part of his journey to the UK.

Victim of trafficking

Louisa left the Dominican Republic when she was 17 because she was offered work in Argentina. Louisa was taken to an apartment where there were many girls working as prostitutes. She tried to leave, but she owed money for the airfare. Luckily, an international agency helped to get Louisa back home.

19

WAR AND IMMIGRATION

Many people escape from countries at war. In the First and Second World Wars, most of the people who died were soldiers. Today however, most of the people injured or killed are just innocent people nearby.

People try to escape from the violence. They also leave because war brings poverty and hunger. Today, most wars take place in the world's poorest nations.

These are some of the countries involved in war (between countries) and civil war (within a country) between 1997 and 2007.

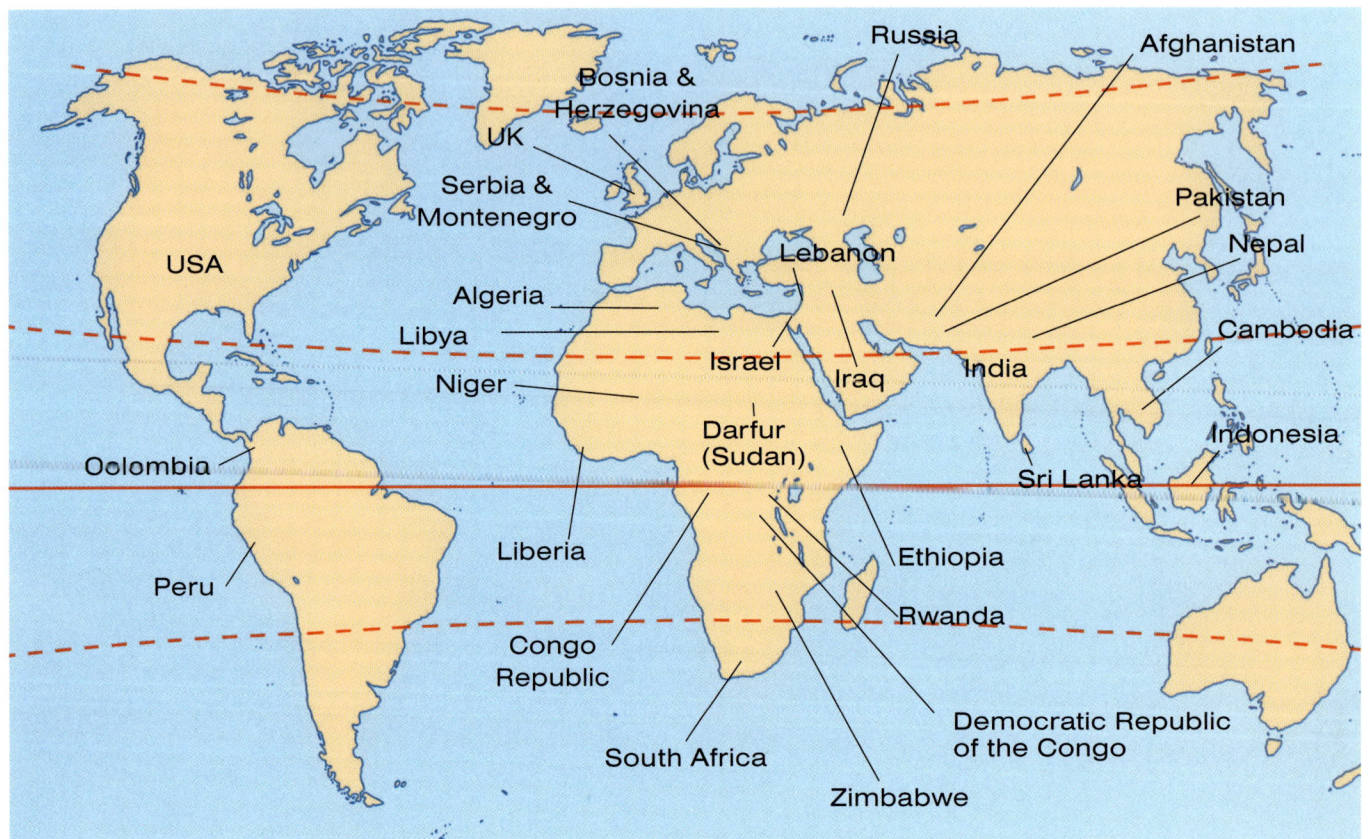

ESCAPING WAR

People who escape a country during a war are in danger. Often, they have to leave their belongings and have no idea where they should travel to. Most people try to get across the nearest border to safety.

Often the journey is dangerous. In 2002, for example, around 65,000 Sudanese refugees went to eastern Chad. They walked for days during the rainy season. During the journey they were also targeted by gunfire from aircraft.

War can destroy towns and cities, causing people to run away.

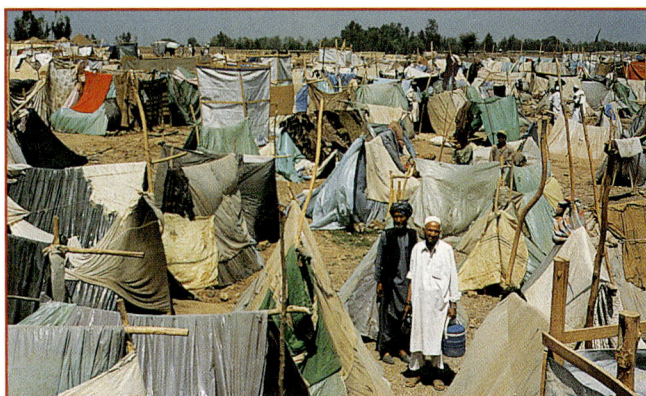

Refugee camps aren't always safe places to stay.

REFUGEE CAMPS

Millions of refugees end up in refugee camps in nearby countries. Some camps are not officially recognised. Others are set up by governments and aid agencies to provide food, water and shelter. Some camps teach people important life skills.

21

Some camps are well organised, but in others, people are very poor. They arrive with nothing but the clothes they're wearing. Some camps are controlled by armed forces, but in others there is little law and order. There are only three ways out – to be able to go home one day; to be allowed to stay in the new country; or to be helped to move on to another country.

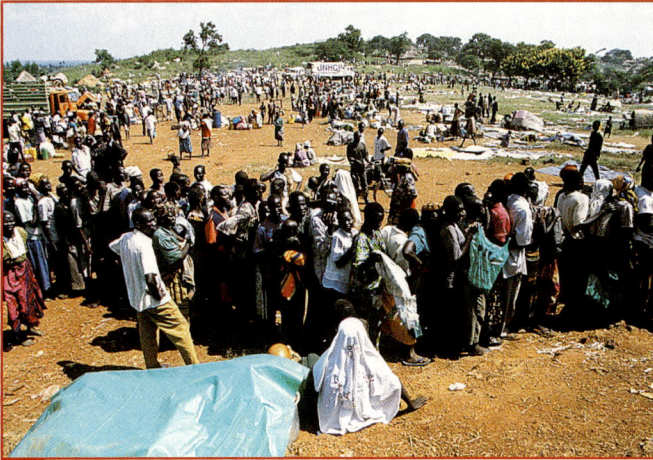

Refugee camps can be very overcrowded. There is often little law and order.

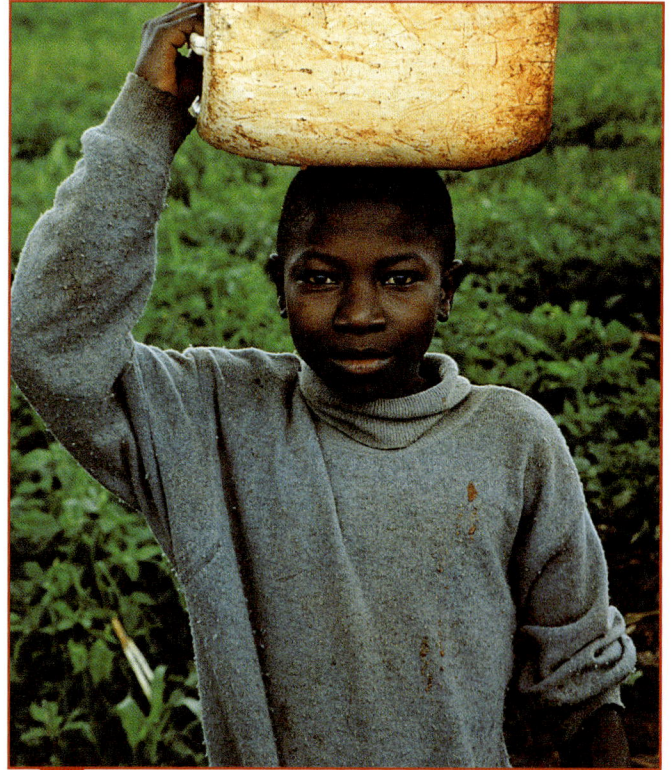

Thousands of Burundians have escaped to Tanzania.

LIVING IN A CAMP

Azerbaijan has 750,000 refugees living there. The country is fighting with Armenia for control of Nagorno Karabakh. This is where the refugees have come from.

The camps are in a terrible condition. Most have tents or temporary huts made from scrap materials. In winter, the camps become a sea of mud. The buildings are overcrowded. They have no running water or sewage systems and very little electricity. Health care is basic and many people become ill because they have a poor diet. Some people have been in the camps for seven years.

TANZANIAN REFUGEES

Tanzania has thousands of refugees from neighbouring countries:

• 300,000 Burundians have fled to Tanzania to escape from civil war.
• 120,000 refugees are from the Democratic Republic of the Congo.
• In the 1990s, half a million Rwandans escaped to Tanzania, although some have now returned.

Tanzania has its own problems, however. Droughts and floods have affected farming and there is not enough food to go round.

22

CHILD SOLDIERS

There are about 300,000 child soldiers around the world. They have been forced to join armies and rebel groups. Some children escape from the violence, but it is hard for them to find a safe place.

Some children in Sierra Leone are forced to work as soldiers.

AVOIDING WAR

Every country has the right to ask its people to fight for them in times of war. This is called conscription. However, people also have the right to refuse if they believe war is wrong. In some countries, people are treated very badly if they don't want to fight.

WAR CRIMINALS

Terrible crimes are committed in wars. The UN has made laws about what can and cannot be done, but these laws are often broken.

People who carry out war crimes are criminals. If their side is losing, some escape by pretending to be ordinary refugees.

23

Refugee rights

The 1951 Geneva Convention, which outlines refugee law, does not include people fleeing from war. However, the UNHCR (see page 46) says that people escaping war should be thought of as refugees if they are loyal to their country.

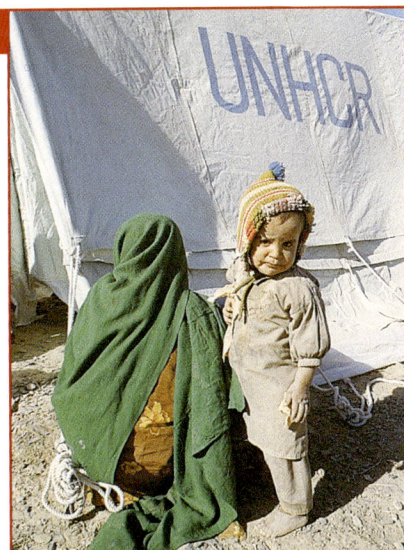

Refugee camps are meant to look after genuine refugees, not war criminals.

RACE AND IMMIGRATION

Today, most countries have mixed populations which include people from different races and ethnic groups.

Most schools in the UK have pupils from many different ethnic backgrounds.

Proportion of people from minority groups

More than 50%	Afghanistan, India, Indonesia, Iran, Kazakhstan, Peru.
30-50%	Bangladesh, Brazil, Colombia, Mexico, Morocco, Malawi, Malaysia, Pakistan.
10-29%	Canada, Russia, South Africa, USA, Zimbabwe.
Less than 10%	Australia, China, Egypt, Japan, UK.

STIRRING UP HATRED

Most of the time, ethnic groups live together peacefully. But political leaders can stir up hatred between groups in order to gain more power. They encourage people to feel threatened by anyone who is different.

In some countries, minority groups have limited rights. This can lead to civil war and even genocide (the killing of a particular group of people). Many people escape to find safety in other countries.

LOOKING FOR SAFETY

People escaping violence do not always find safety in a new country. Roma people fleeing Kosovo, for example, face difficulties in many places. Sometimes, immigrants find that they are hated in a new country.

Since 2002, for example, about a quarter of the citizens in Côte d'Ivoire, have been abused because their relatives are immigrants. Migration is becoming more common, but sometimes groups of people like to make people afraid of immigration.

When racism leads to immigration.

Bhutan
In the early 1990s, more than 100,000 people were forced to leave Bhutan. The refugees have been living in camps in south-eastern Nepal ever since.

Rwanda
In the mid-1990s, Tutsis and Hutus who opposed the Hutu government were violently killed. Around 800,000 people lost their lives and nearly two million Rwandans tried to escape the country.

Iraq
For 23 years, Saddam Hussein ordered the capture and torture of Kurds in northern Iraq. The Shi'a community and other minority groups were also treated very badly.

Bosnia-Herzegovina
In a period of 'ethnic cleansing', Serbian forces killed, raped and terrorised ethnic groups in Bosnia-Herzegovina in the 1990s Many escaped to other countries (below).

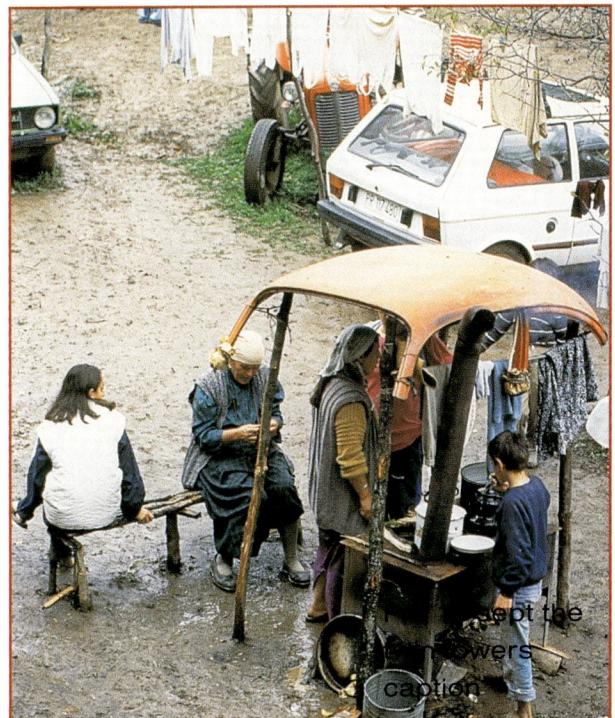

25

POLITICS AND IMMIGRATION

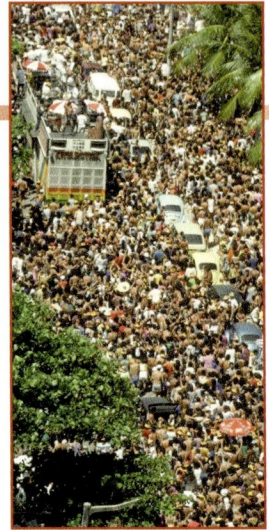

Most people migrate to have a better way of life. Countries that have a good government tend to be richer, but many people move to countries with bad governments, too.

Asylum seekers are often forced to leave countries where the government is bad or weak. Some may be political leaders themselves. Others may not agree with the government and may need to escape to avoid being arrested.

Thousands of Zimbabweans have escaped from the rule of the president, Robert Mugabe.

ZIMBABWE

President Robert Mugabe has ruled Zimbabwe for more than 20 years. He is a very bad leader. In 2002, his government ordered a campaign against people who opposed the government. Many people say they have been beaten and tortured. The government also made sure that people who opposed the government would have limited access to food supplies.

CHINA

China is becoming a very successful country. However, hundreds of people are killed every year in China because they oppose the government. People are imprisoned very easily and there are laws about the publication of books, magazines, websites and televisions programmes. In 2000, around 18,000 people escaped from China to seek asylum in Europe.

EAST TIMOR

East Timor used to belong to Portugal. A political leader called José Ramos-Horta campaigned for the country's independence. In 1974, when the Portuguese left, Ramos-Horta was made a government minister. However, Indonesia invaded the following year while Ramos-Horta was away. This meant that he could not go back. Ramos-Horta spent the next 23 years speaking out against the Indonesian occupation. He helped to get a peace plan started and in 2002, East Timor became an independent country once again.

Foreign-born politicians

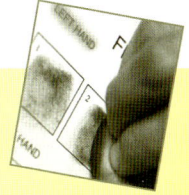

Arnold Schwarzenegger is Austrian but he moved to the USA in 1970 to became a film star. He became a US citizen in 1984 and was elected governor of California in 2003.

Madeleine Albright is the former Secretary of State for the USA. Her family fled from their home in Czechoslovakia to escape the Nazis.

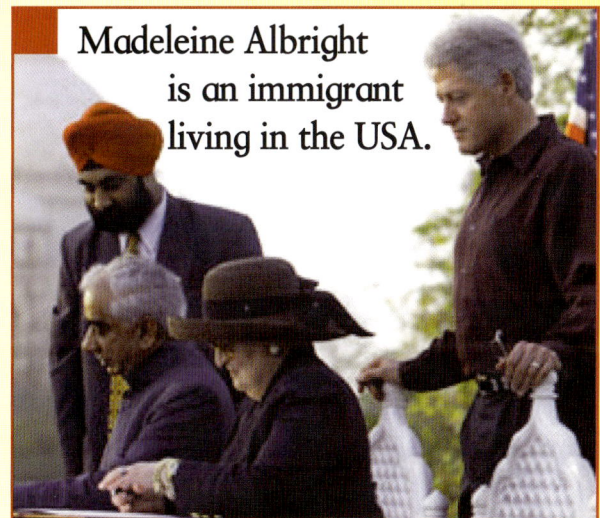

Madeleine Albright is an immigrant living in the USA.

They went to the UK and were then granted asylum in the USA. Albright later became a US citizen.

These are two successful politicians. However, at the moment, neither of them could become President of the United States because they were not born in the USA.

27

RELIGION AND IMMIGRATION

Over the centuries, religions have spread around the world as people have moved. During the Second World War, about six million Jews were killed by the Nazis. Thousands of Jews escaped and when the country Israel was created, many people moved there. Religion causes some people to be very much against immigration.

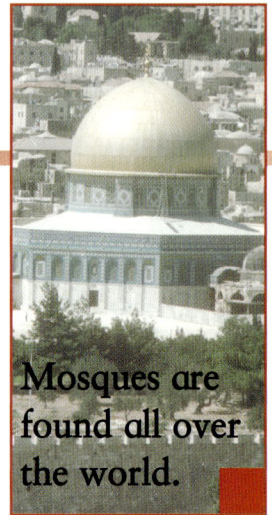

Mosques are found all over the world.

Sikhism is a religion from India that is now practised in many parts of the world.

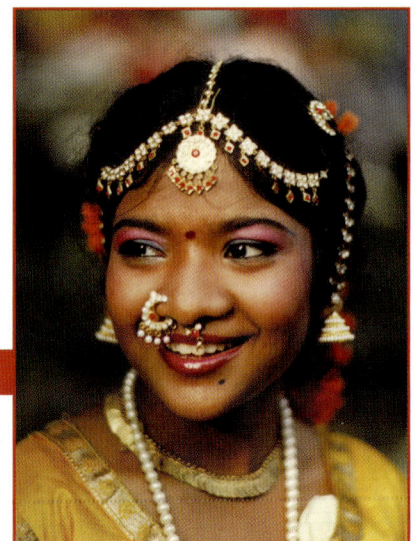

Hindus are the largest religious group in India. Their religion has spread around the world.

The right to believe

The UN Declaration of Human Rights says that everyone has the right to worship and to change their religion or beliefs. However, many people have been forced to leave their country because of their religious beliefs. In 2003, thousands of Hindus fled from Bangladesh to India, because they were being treated badly. Thousands of Bosnian Muslims were also killed or forced from their homes when Serbia invaded.

FINDING A SAFE PLACE

In 2001, members of a Vietnamese hill tribe fled to Cambodia. They claimed their government were taking away their farmland. Known as the Montagnards, they are mostly Christian. Their government had also banned some of their church services.

REBUILDING LIVES

Germany has the world's fastest-growing population of Jewish people. Most come from the former Soviet Union. The old Jewish quarter of Berlin is busy again, but the Jews have also been attacked. Police try to protect them.

FORCED TO RETURN

In the 1990s, about 250,000 Muslim refugees travelled to Bangladesh to escape from difficulties in Burma. Their land had been taken away and they were being treated badly. When the UN tried to help, many people returned to Burma. However, some returned to Bangladesh again, saying the situation had not improved. By 2003, there were 20,000 refugees living in camps in Bangladesh, in difficult conditions.

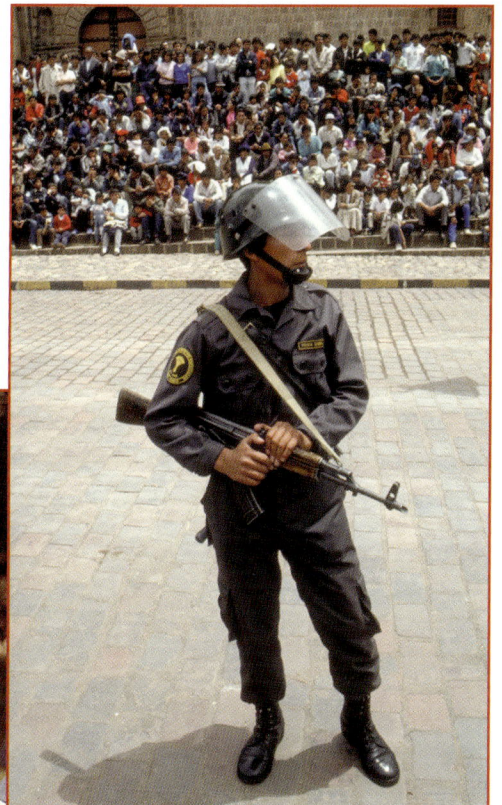

29

After the Second World War many Jews moved to Israel.

In some countries, police are needed to protect certain religious groups.

WOMEN AND IMMIGRATION

Today, many women migrate to other countries. In the past, women usually moved away with their family. The men in the family tried to earn the money they needed. Now, more women are travelling on their own to earn money for their families. In Asia, most of the migrants working overseas are women.

Women migrants are at risk.

Nearly half of migrants in the world are women.

MAKING A LIVING

Migration can be a positive experience for women. Many find a job and gain independence for the first time. But it is not always good news. Because women tend to be paid less than men, women migrants are more likely than men to accept bad working conditions.

Women often work as cooks or cleaners. It is difficult for the government to control the working conditions of these jobs. Some women set up businesses to earn money at home and overseas. Moroccan women in Italy are busy building trading links with their home country, for example.

WOMEN REFUGEES

Around 50% of the world's refugees are women and girls. Most of them have fled their homes because of war. Others are escaping from bad governments. In some countries, women are treated badly because they refuse an arranged marriage, leave a violent husband, or wear the wrong clothes.

Women also suffer particular forms of abuse, such as rape. They may not have the money to arrange travel to a safe country. Many women are tricked by traffickers and smugglers.

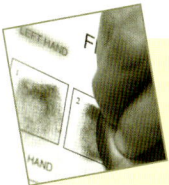

When women flee their homes they are in danger.

From maid to model

Waris Dirie grew up in the Somali desert, but she fled to escape an arranged marriage. She got a job as a maid to the Somali ambassador in London. For four years, she cooked and cleaned for him. When the Ambassador returned to Somalia she hid so she could stay in London. She was hired as a model. This was the start of an international career.

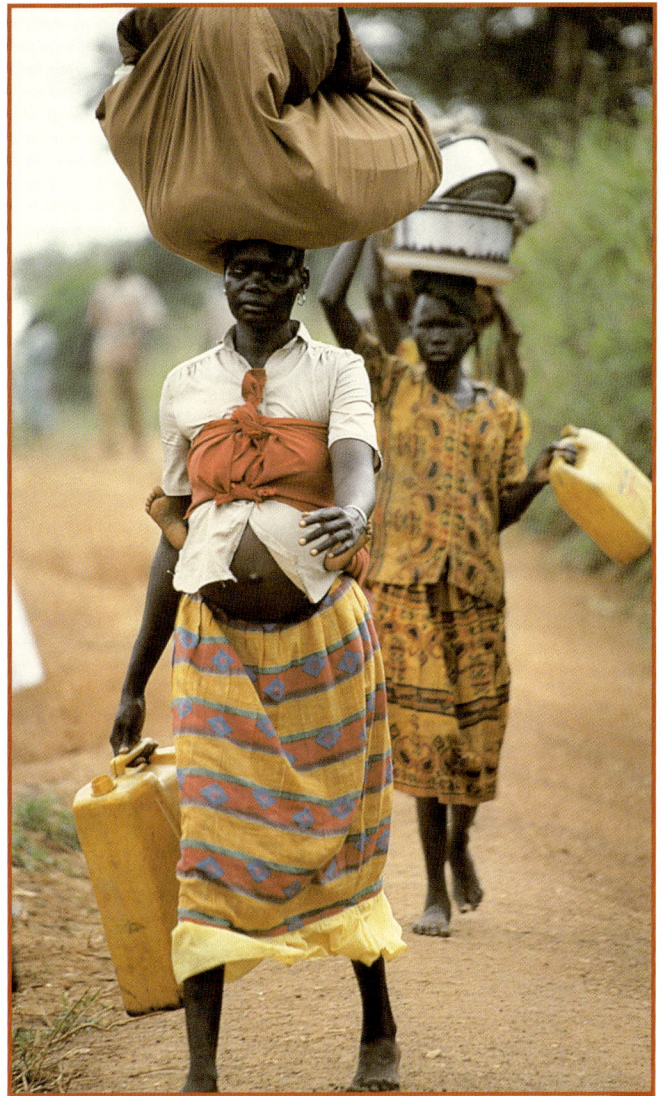

FEMALE TRAFFICKING

Up to two million women and children are victims of traffickers each year. It is not easy for them to escape. Sometimes, they manage to run away. However, the authorities treat them as illegal immigrants, and may send them back to where they came from.

31

CHILDREN AND IMMIGRATION

Sometimes, children move because their parents are going to work abroad. Other children are sent on their own to stay with relatives. Some children are trying to escape from violence.

YOUNG IMMIGRANTS

Many children arrive in a country legally, to live with an adult who cares for them. Some governments run schemes that help to bring relatives together.

Some children have to travel to a faraway country on their own.

A website creator

Sieng Van Tran's family fled from Vietnam when he was three. Tran went to school and university in the UK. Later, he created a website that gives people the chance to learn from home. He called the project 'iLearn.To'. He asked a team of financial backers to invest US$4.5 million in the website. He is now on his way to becoming a multi-millionaire.

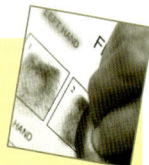

YOUNG REFUGEES

Around half the world's refugees are children. Some children escape on their own, but may not find protection in another country. In Canada, about 50% of child asylum seekers are officially recognised as refugees. In Europe, only 5% are. However, often more children are allowed to stay, to prevent them from suffering further.

CHILD TRAFFICKING

Trafficked children are made to work for very little or no money. Children can also be forced to work in the sex industry.

These children are abused and their health suffers. The traffickers make a lot of money and they are rarely caught. Parents often think their child is being looked after, but they may never hear from their child again.

REASONS TO ESCAPE

Children become refugees to escape danger. Their family may be treated badly because of their race, religion or political beliefs. Their country may be at war. Sometimes, parents send their children away because they think it is safer to do so.

Children's rights

Children can be refugees in their own right and all countries are responsible for a child's safety.

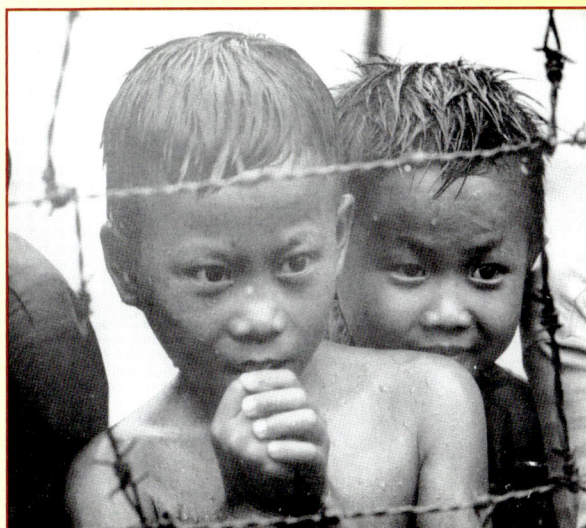

Countries should provide protection and help to children, whether they are with their parents or alone. But some governments don't treat child refugees very well.

33

Many Afghan children are now immigrants in Pakistan.

ENVIRONMENT AND IMMIGRATION

Every year, thousands of people are affected by natural and man-made disasters. These include floods, droughts, earthquakes and forest fires. In the future, climate change will lead to more people escaping environmental problems. Although these people aren't thought to be refugees, they do need help. Some people think that rich countries should provide it.

SINKING ISLAND

Tuvalu is a tiny nation in the Pacific, made up of nine islands. The islands stand only three metres above the waves. Because sea levels are rising, the islanders are slowly leaving. New Zealand has taken some of the refugees. However, in the future, the whole population may have to move overseas.

FAMINE

Up to 300,000 people have fled from famine in North Korea. A bad government and natural disasters have caused over six years of food shortages. This has made life in the country very difficult.

When there is no rain, crops can fail and a country may be at risk of famine.

DANGEROUS AREAS

Waste material from nuclear weapons or nuclear reactors can be very dangerous. After the break-up of the Soviet Union in 1990, the new countries had to deal with a lot of radioactive waste material. At least 700,000 people have moved away from dangerous areas.

A GROWING DESERT

In many dry parts of the world, the ground is slowly becoming like a desert. People are trying to farm and live off the land, but very little will grow.

Millions of people in Africa may have to leave these dry areas in the next 20 years. Many have already left because they can't grow enough food. Poverty, drought and lack of water is making the situation worse. The problem is also caused by cutting down too many trees.

VOLCANIC ERUPTION

In 1997, a volcano on the island of Montserrat erupted. Fortunately, many people had left the south of the island because of an eruption a few months earlier. In 1998, nearly half of Montserrat's 11,000 population had to leave the island because their homes had been destroyed. Many went to the UK.

35

Although Montserrat was badly damaged, many people have now returned home.

WHAT GOVERNMENTS DO

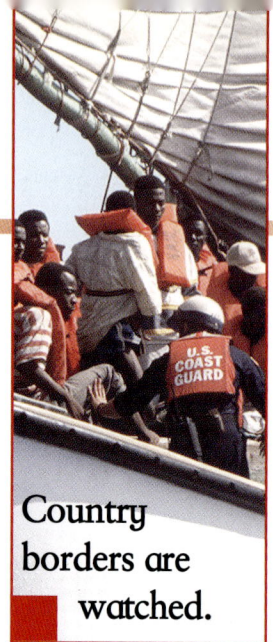

Country borders are watched.

Governments have become aware of the increasing number of immigrants. Some try to limit the number of people crossing borders. But some people think the reasons behind immigration need to be addressed.

? Reasons to take control

The economy – Immigration can benefit a country, but only if it is well managed.

For security – To limit international crime and terrorist attacks.

To secure votes – Immigration is now a hot political issue.

To stop extremist groups – Anti-immigrant and racist groups should be prevented from acting.

To meet international laws – Most governments have to offer safety to refugees and to respect the rights of immigrants.

A FEW SOLUTIONS

• Monitoring international flights and strengthening border controls.
• Carrying out police raids.
• Sending illegal immigrants home.
• Introducing identity cards.
• Cutting back financial aid for asylum seekers.
• Punishing employers who use illegal labourers, and punishing smugglers and traffickers.
• Closing refugee camps.

Sniffer dogs help to find immigrants crossing borders.

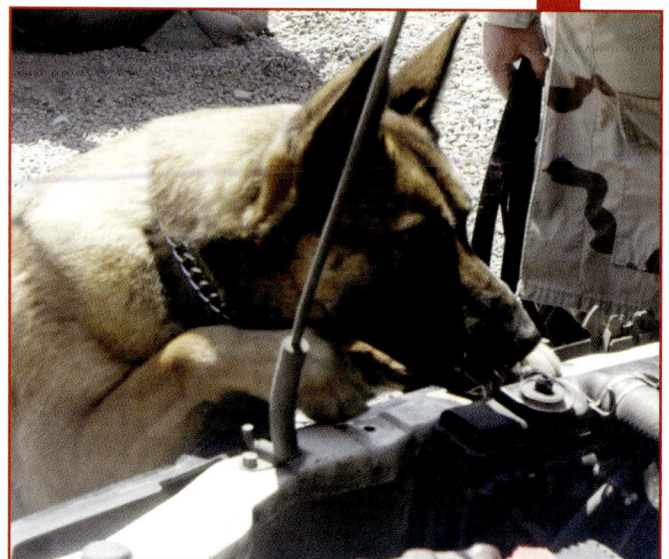

36

OPPOSITE VIEWS

Human rights groups do not like immigration controls. They say that countries benefit from immigrants.

When immigration is restricted, people try to enter a country illegally. Genuine refugees suffer and try to be smuggled in as a way to escape. Human rights groups want more investment in countries of emigration. They also want aid to help people overcome poverty, so they don't have to move away.

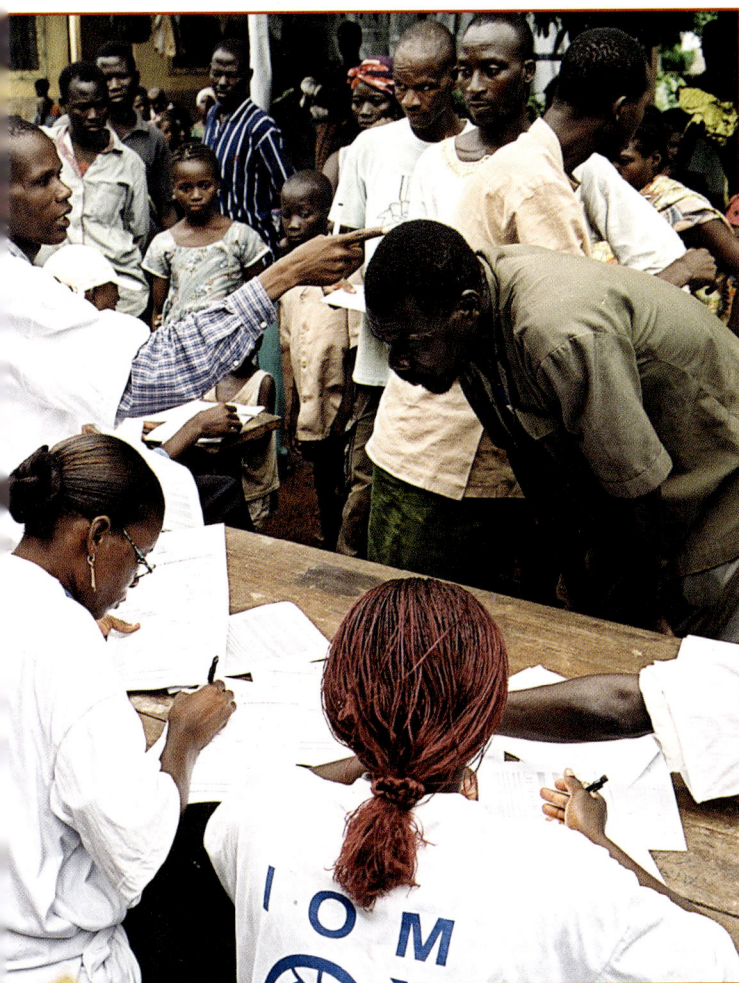

LEGAL MIGRATION

Sometimes governments encourage immigration. In the 1950s, for example, London Transport employed staff from the West Indies to work on buses and underground trains. Countries that have encouraged permanent migration include the USA, Israel, Australia and New Zealand.

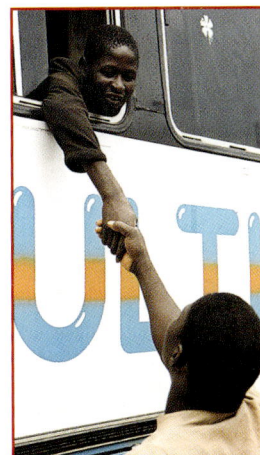

INTERNATIONAL AID

Governments have to work together to manage migration. Many governments provide aid directly to countries that migrants are leaving. Some offer more help when there is a major disaster. Most governments support the UN and international aid agencies in their work to fight poverty and to help refugees.

The International Organisation for Migration works with refugees all over the world.

37

Migrants wait outside the Sangatte refugee camp in France.

SANGATTE, FRANCE

The Sangatte refugee camp in northern France became famous as a place for migrants trying to reach the UK. However, there were a number of problems. French shop-keepers did not like refugees hanging around in the town. Many refugees also tried to enter the nearby Channel Tunnel at night in an attempt to reach the UK. This disrupted many trains.

The rail company asked for the camp to be shut down. Sangatte was closed in 2002, after the French and British governments agreed that half the camp's residents would be allowed into the UK. The others were encouraged to go home (or were sent back). But new migrants continued to arrive.

Preventing movement

• Botswana has put up a fence to prevent migrants from Zimbabwe.
• The Australian navy has stopped boats carrying refugees to prevent them landing on its shores. These people are put into refugee camps.
• After the September 11 terrorist attacks in the USA, many men from Arab countries living in the USA had to have their papers checked.

38

WHAT IMMIGRANTS DO

Many migrants end up doing difficult and dangerous jobs, which are badly paid. Illegal immigrants are more likely to be treated badly than legal immigrants.

TYPES OF WORK

Immigrants often work in the following areas:

Building work – Many immigrants work on building sites. The work is often hard and dangerous.

Agriculture – Farms need seasonal workers to pick the harvest. Much of this work is done by hand.

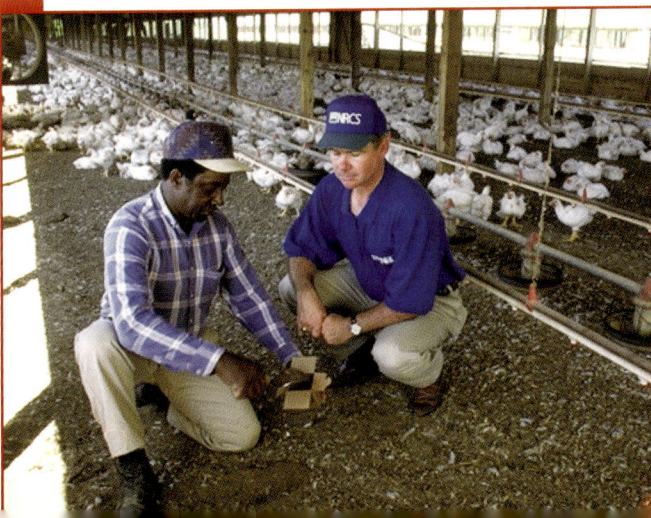

Work done by immigrants can be very dangerous.

Personal services – Jobs that range from nursing and childcare to cleaning and gardening.

Factories – Legal immigrants may work in factories with good working conditions. Others end up in small factories that have terrible working conditions.

Many immigrants work in farming.

At one time, these jobs would have been done by women and children. But in developed countries, women have become better educated. There are fewer babies being born, and not enough young people to do low-paid work.

Singapore

Since the 1960s, there have not been enough people to work in Singapore. The country needs immigrants to fill jobs. In the 1990s, there were more than 300,000 migrants in Singapore.

Immigrants are important to the country, but the lower-paid workers face many problems. Bad working conditions affect their health. Many migrants are also trying to pay off the cost of moving to Singapore. Illegal immigrants, in particular, often do not earn enough to survive.

40

CROP-PICKING

Over 100,000 migrants work for gangs on farms and in the food packing industry in the UK. The government knows that without these workers, the industry would collapse. Most workers live and work in the UK illegally.

In February 2004, 19 Chinese migrant workers drowned whilst picking cockles in Morecambe Bay, in the UK. They were caught by the dangerous fast-rising tide. Their employers had made them work in very dangerous conditions.

A CAREER MOVE

Educated and professional people often become international migrants. They move to cities where they can develop their careers.

This is not all bad news, however. Some people return to their home country years later, with better skills and more experience.

Thousands of professional people migrate each year in search of a better job.

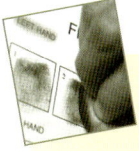

Working to live

Tran and Lam are Vietnamese refugees living in Australia. They work with their four children for long hours, making clothes for large companies. Their employers always push for the work to be done more quickly. The pay is in cash. By working long hours, the family has just enough to live on.

MAKING MONEY

Migrants send money home. They also spend money in their new country. In 2001, Mexicans living in the USA sent about US$9 billion to Mexico. The rest (about 85 per cent) of their income they spent locally. The Mexicans help to generate about US$82 billion dollars a year for the USA!

Many companies employ foreign-born workers.

41

USEFUL PROFESSIONALS

The UK's National Health Service (NHS) is one of the largest employers in Europe. The NHS finds workers from overseas because there is a shortage of British doctors and nurses. This is useful but there are fears that standards of care might drop.

Leaving home

Abel is a doctor working in Zimbabwe. He wants to move to Australia where he could earn a lot more. Since 1980, more than 80 per cent of health graduates from the University of Zimbabwe have gone to work abroad.

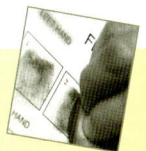

GOING HOME

Some people are able to return home.

Twenty years ago, most immigrants moved to a new country where they spent the rest of their lives. Now it is more complicated. People travel to work abroad for a short amount of time. Sometimes, a family moves overseas, but the grandchildren move back again.

Going back to Kosovo

Zoran is one of nearly 200,000 Serbs and Romas who fled Kosovo in 1999. In 2003, he went back to his village. As more people returned, the village began to feel like home again. Aid agencies have helped with food supplies and repairs.

RETURNING REFUGEES

Many refugees hope to go home when their country is safe. The journey can be expensive, and they often have to rebuild their lives. Sometimes, the situation they return to is still difficult. Often, aid agencies work closely with governments to make travel arrangements and to set up work and housing programmes.

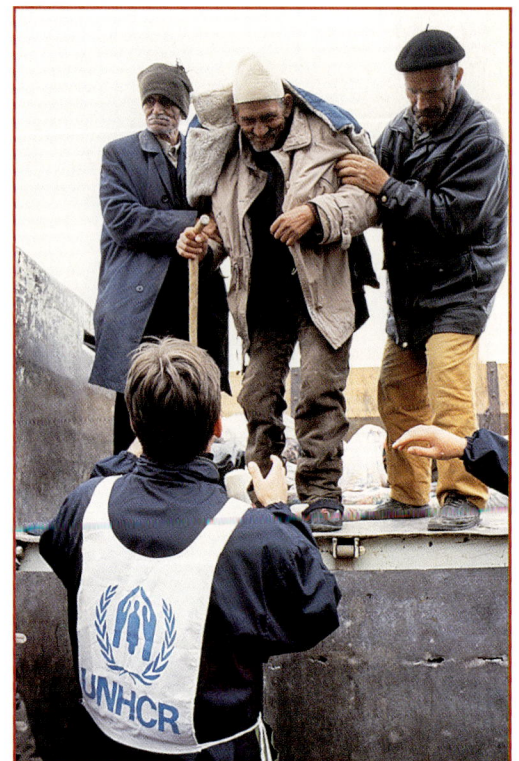
The UNHCR helps refugees to return to their home country.

42

NEW PLACE, NEW HOME

While many people go back to their home country, others never return. Many people find jobs or start to raise a family. Some people apply to be 'citizens' of the country they move to. This means they can vote in elections, and they have the same rights and responsibilities as other people.

Famous migrants

Throughout history, immigrants have changed our world. J F Kennedy, the youngest US president, was descended from Irish great-grandparents. Other famous refugees include Salvador Dali (artist), Edward Said (academic, see page 17), and Frederic Chopin (composer).

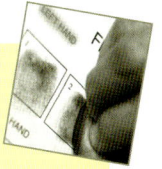

Many migrants want to return home to live without fear.

43

FORCED TO RETURN

Many asylum seekers and illegal immigrants are sent back to their country. Sometimes an asylum application is turned down. Other people are sent home because they don't have official documents. Some people are badly treated in the country they go back to.

Many governments are tightening their border controls. In 2002, many western European countries sent Chechen asylum seekers home, claiming that conditions in their country had improved. Human rights groups said the conditions were still dangerous, however.

CHRONOLOGY

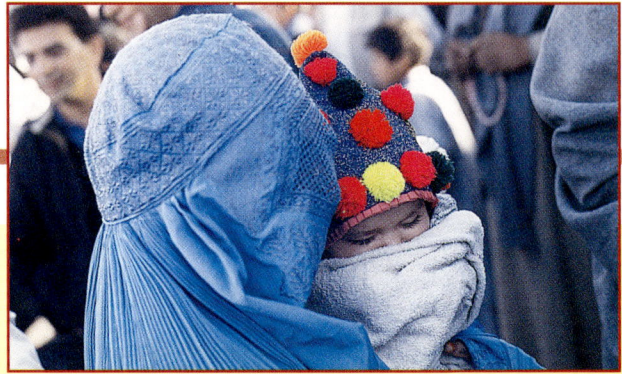

400 BC-500 AD – The Roman Empire spread over large parts of Europe. Christians escaped from the Roman-occupied countries, where they were treated badly.

800-1100 – Vikings (Nordic people) moved across Europe from Scandinavia. Some of them even got as far as North America.

1492 – Christopher Columbus reached the Americas. This was the start of mass immigration as Europeans moved to America.

Late 1400s-1865 – Around 15 million Africans were taken to America and forced to work as slaves.

Early 1600s – Many immigrants crossed from Europe to North America. The journey took 6-12 weeks and many people died of disease.

1620 – The Mayflower ship crossed the Atlantic from Plymouth, England, to Cape Cod in North America. The ship carried 102 passengers, known as the Pilgrims.

Late 1600s-1800s – Thousands of Protestants escaped from France to America and Europe, because they were being treated very badly.

1788-1868 – Around 162,000 convicts (prisoners) were sent to Australia from England and Ireland.

1807 – Britain banned the slave trade.

1820-1924 – Around 35-40 million Europeans moved to America, looking for a better way of life.

1846-1850 – The Irish Potato Famine caused the emigration of up to two million people.

1917-1925 – Around 1.5 million people left Russia to escape communism, starvation and war.

1930-1942 – Over 300,000 Jews left German-occupied countries.

1947 – India was divided (into India and Pakistan), causing large-scale emigration. Many moved to the UK.

1948 – Israel was created and Jews moved there from Europe.

1948 – The UN agreed the Universal Declaration of Human Rights. This law gives everyone the right to seek asylum in other countries, for example.

1960 onwards – Many immigrant workers brought their families to live with them in Western countries.

1980 – Around 8.2 million refugees and displaced people worldwide.

1989 – The fall of the Berlin Wall caused the migration of around 218,000 Germans from Eastern Europe to Germany.

1989-1994 – Around 700,000 refugees from the former Yugoslavia fled to Western Europe.

1991 – The Gulf War. Nearly two million people fled to neighbouring countries from Iraq.

1995 – Around 26 million refugees and displaced people worldwide.

2002 – US approvals for asylum fell by 72% due to strict controls after the 2001 terrorist attacks.

Mid 2002-Mid 2003 – Up to 1.5 million West Africans were forced to leave their homes because of war.

2003 – Around 20 million refugees and displaced people worldwide.

2003 – Between January and September, the largest group of asylum seekers were from Russia.

2003-2007 – At least 200,000 people were killed in a civil war in Sudan's Darfur region. More than two million people were displaced.

2004 and 2007 – New countries of the European Union increased the control of their borders to prevent illegal immigrants from entering.

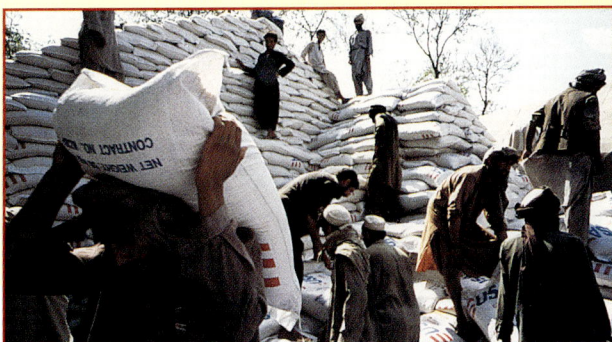

45

ORGANISATIONS AND GLOSSARY

Anti-Slavery International
www.antislavery.org
Works at local, national and international levels to prevent slavery around the world.

Canadian Council for Refugees
www.web.net/~ccr/
Tries to protect refugees in Canada and around the world. It also helps refugees and immigrants to live and work in Canada.

Human Rights Watch
www.hrw.org
Protects the human rights of people worldwide. They investigate and follow up examples of human rights abuse. They ask governments to respect international human rights law.

International Organisation for Migration (IOM)
www.iom.int
Works to increase understanding of migration issues. Encourages support for immigrants and development for countries through increased migration.

National Network for Immigrant and Refugee Rights (NNIRR)
www.nnirr.org
A national organisation made up of immigrant, refugee and other organisations.

Refugee Council
www.refugeecouncil.org.uk

Refugee Council of Australia
www.refugeecouncil.org.au

Sweatshop Watch
www.sweatshopwatch.org
Tries to stop the exploitation of workers in sweatshops.

United Nations High Commissioner for Refugees (UNHCR)
www.unhcr.ch
The main agency for the protection of displaced people and refugees.

Other useful websites:

www.bbc.co.uk
News items on migration and refugees around the world.

www.movinghere.org.uk
Interactive website about 200 years of migration to the UK.

www.endchildexploitation.org.uk
A campaign to end child exploitation.

Aid – Money or support given to countries in need.

Asylum – Shelter from danger.

Asylum seeker – Someone seeking safety or refugee status in another country.

Border – The boundary of a country.

Citizen – A person who has a legal right to live in a country and be protected by its laws.

Developed countries – Countries that are wealthy and advanced.

Developing countries – Countries in the process of being industrialised.

Drought – When there is no rainfall and crops are unable to grow.

Economy – The financial situation in a country.

Emigration – When people leave a country.

Human rights – The basic rights that we should all have. These include the right to life, the right to freedom and the right to fair treatment before the law.

Illegal immigrant – Someone who lives in another country illegally.

Immigrant – Someone who has moved to a country in order to live there, and who would like to stay for a while.

Immigration – The process of people crossing borders in order to stay in a foreign country.

Migration – The movement of people from one area or country.

Poverty – Being poor and not having access to basic needs such as education, jobs and healthcare.

Race – People who come from the same ethnic group.

Racism – Discriminating against people on the basis of their skin colour or ethnic origin.

Refugee – Someone who has fled their country and has been granted asylum in another country.

Smuggler – Someone who gets people across borders illegally.

Trafficking – Moving people to make money, often by force.

47

Index

Photo Credits:
Abbreviations: l-left, r-right, b-bottom, t-top, c-centre, m-middle
Front cover main, 4bl, 15tr, 31tr, 33br — UNHCR/A. Hollmann. 1ml, 18tl — Thomas Michael Corcoran/USMC. 1c, 7ml, 8bl — Eric Eggen/USCG. 1mr — Flat Earth. 2bl — Sarah Foster-Snell/USCG. 2-3b — Robin Ressler/USCG. 3tr, 11br, 23br, 30 both, 44tr — UNHCR. 4mr — Ken Hammond/USDA. 5tl, 22tl, 45bl — UNHCR/S. Mann. 5tr — © IOM 1983-HTH0131. 6tr — © IOM 2002-MKE0002-Photo: Sasha Chanoff. 6bl — Don Wagner/USCG. 7mt, 8tr, 15mb, 24ml, 40 both — Corbis. 9tl — © Tessa Nylan-MKE0121-Photo: Tessa Nylan. 10bl, 11tl, 20tr, 21bl, 26tr, 28tr, 28ml, 28mr, 29mr, 39mr, 42tr — Corel. 12t — © IOM 1999-MID0001-Photo: Christopher Lowenstein-Lom. 12tr — © IOM 2003-MJO0056- Jean-Philippe Chauzny. 5bl, 12bl, 13c, 14br, 16ml, 19bl, 23bl, 27tr, 28bl, 31ml, 32c, 33tr, 38br, 41tl, 41br, 42ml, 43tr — Photodisc. 13ml, 13br —PBD. 14tr — © IOM 2002-MAF0101-Photo: Jeff Labovitz. 14bl — © IOM 2002-MCH0023-Photo: Thomas Moran. 16tr — © IOM 1999-MTR0010. 17br — Galen Rowell/CORBIS. 18mr, 38mr — UNHCR/H. J. Davies. 19tr — U.S. Border Patrol. 21tr — UNHCR/C. Shirley. 22tr — UNHCR/L. Taylor. 23ml — UNHCR/C. Sattlberger. 24tr — Ken Hammond/USDA. 25br — UNHCR/R. LeMoyne. 26bl — Rob Cooper/CORBIS SYGMA. 27mr — U. S. National Archives & Records Administration. 29bl — © IOM 1999-MID0001-Photo: Christopher Lowenstein-Lom. 32tr — U. S. Coast Guard. 33mr — © IOM 1979-HTH0031-Photo: Karl Zirbs. 34br — UNHCR/M. Vacca. 35tl — Comstock. 35br — Bernhard Edmaier/Science Photo Library. 36tr — Steve Sapp/USCG. 36br — Matthew J. Apprendi/USMC. 37tr — © IOM 2003-MCI0017-Photo: Jean-Philippe Chauzny. 37bl — © IOM 2003-MCI0004-Photo: Jean-Philippe Chauzny. 38t — Roininen Juha/CORBIS SYGMA. 39bl — Bob Nichols/USDA. 41c — Lauren Hobart/FEMA. 42br — UNHCR/P. Benatar. 43c — © IOM 1999-MTP0009-Photo: Christopher Lowenstein-Lom. 45tr — © IOM 1956-HFG0237.